COAL FLOWERS

MEMORIES OF A PAISLEY CHILDHOOD

BY

DONALD MALCOLM

To my beautiful little grand-daughter
Hannah Margaret Malcolm
newly minted, dreaming dreams

First published in the United Kingdom 1996
by
Richard Stenlake Publishing
Ochiltree Sawmill, The Lade,
Ochiltree, Ayrshire
KA18 2NX
Tel/Fax 01290 423114

ISBN 1 872074 81 2

TELEPHONE Nº 14.

TIMBER STORED
AND SAWN TO ORDER
WHEN REQUIRED·

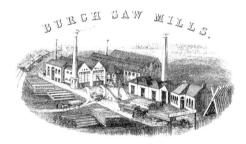

BURGH SAW MILLS,

CALEDONIA STREET,

PAISLEY.

Previous page: Me, aged four, at the door of my mother's confectioner and tobacconist shop at 58 Canal Street, 1934.

INTRODUCTION

Writers always have plenty of ideas. Some are never used, others are developed quickly and a few lie around for years, awaiting the spark that will ignite them to life.

The idea behind this little book comes into the last category. Garnered over a long period of time, I had scribbled notes on incidents of my life and times in a Paisley tenement; but mostly they remained in my mind. My working title was *A Tenement Childhood*. However, it was used by someone else, hence the title under which the publication appears.

Not having the faculty of total recall, I have written only about what I can honestly remember. Where the recollection is a half-memory, I have said so. Hindsight has enabled me to see and to understand some things that were not so clear when I was nearer to events and not given to introspection. Remembering is rather like striking a flint - little slivers of light amid the darkness. This book may help to make these memories a little less ephemeral.

I have tried to give a picture of life in a tenement and its environs in a light-hearted way, and I am the first to laugh at myself. (Don't look for *Cider With Rosie, Catcher in the Rye* or a Dirk Bogarde autobiography.) You, the reader, will decide whether or not I have succeeded.

Donald Malcolm, 1996

BEGINNINGS

I was born within sound of H.G. Wells (his home was nearby), at Ilford in Essex. Strangely, I have no memory of the place where I lived for the first three years of my life, nor, sadly, of my natural parents, Roland and Nellie Hall. I was officially adopted by John and Elizabeth Malcolm on 11th April 1934 and I took the high road to Scotland.

My first memory is of lying, probably in the cot used to transport me, in a railway station likely to have been Glasgow Central. Above me stood a man holding a giant teddy bear, which I still have. That was probably my adoptive father.

My first home in Paisley was at 58 Canal Street, where my mother had a confectioner's shop on the corner of what was then West Buchanan Street. I have photographs taken at the shop door. If you stand at the foot of Camphill Brae, on the same side as the Fire Station, then walk to the middle of the road, there you'll meet my ghost from sixty years ago.

Upstairs, behind the house, which was two-storey like most of the houses on that side of the street, was a joinery owned by a Mr MacArthur who rejoiced in the very unlikely nickname of 'Spongerina'. In later years I asked my father the origin of it but he didn't know. I had the run of the workshop, full of gleaming tools, including a circular saw, and pungent with the wonderful fragrances of beech and pine and ankle-deep wood shavings. The only time that I came to grief in that potentially dangerous place was when I made a crude wooden sword which I proceeded to get stuck down my throat. The local chemist found me and carried me, sword and all, round to his shop in George Street before removing the offending weapon. Looking back, I cannot help thinking that it would never have happened to Errol Flynn.

As you looked across the road to Camphill Brae, on the right-hand corner there was another confectioner, my mother's rival with whom she was engaged in a bloodless battle for the pennies of the Camphill School pupils. On the left-hand corner was a butcher's shop. At that time, we had a beautiful big half-Persian cat, Billy, and also his pal, a crotchety cairn terrier called Grumphy. The name suited him, but it didn't mean what you probably think it does. The mother had gone into a pig sty to have her litter

4

and a grumphy was a young pig. The two together were a kind of Butch and Sundance of the animal world. We had a miniature wicker basket which the dog carried in his mouth and the intrepid pair crossed the road to the butcher, who put some scraps in it and back they came.

On the same side as our shop, on the farther side of West Buchanan Street, was a dairy where we used to get provisions. It was here one day that I apparently embarked on a life of crime. I was coming back with a bottle of milk when I dropped it. There happened to be one of those massive Highland policemen on the spot. I can't remember what he said, if anything, but he did give me a belt on the left ear. I never could fathom how that was supposed to solve anything, but it was just one of the many unaccountable actions adults inflicted on children. Think what a furore such an incident would provoke today. What with the police, the wooden sword and the circular saw, I would have been a social worker's idea of heaven and would have been headline news in the *Paisley Express*. Until now, I hadn't realised that I'd led such an adventurous life from an early age.

Sometime in 1935 I was enrolled in the prestigious John Neilson Institution - the Porridge Bowl - which, as a listed building converted to superior housing, still dominates with an elegant magnificence the hill at West Brae. (My schooling was to be the subject of another adult decision - see on.) It was while I was in Primary in the J.N.I that another 'assault' took place, by my teacher, Miss Marr. I can say now that she was fully justified in her action. Early on, it was evident that I was lazy and that I was seldom going to treat school as seriously as I should have done. On that occasion my head was bounced off the oak desk. When my mother inquired about the incident, Miss Marr explained in exasperation that I had it in me, but that I wouldn't try.

By 1936, we had moved from Canal Street to 30 Wellmeadow, in the shadow of the Neilson. My mother might have given up the shop, I'm not sure and my father worked as a flesher, as butchers were sometimes called (although there might have been a distinction). The house can be seen on Edwardian postcards but later the site was taken by a Galbraith's shop, and today by an Indian restaurant.

Only four things come to mind about what must have been a fairly short stay in Wellmeadow. Perhaps my mother still had the shop, because what was then termed a 'commercial traveller' used to call at the house. He was a very smartly-dressed man, with a moustache and what I think was a trilby hat. His shoes were among the best-kept and shiniest that I have ever seen, an unusual sight as in those days most men wore boots. One day, he let me into the secrets of caring for quality leather shoes, including how the layers of polish were built up. When he wanted to strip some of the layers off he used a razor blade - with due warning to small boys - and it was fascinating to watch this being done. There was also a man who stayed in the same building who took the greatest pride in his boots and I remember seeing him one day, putting a worn-out pair in the bin, gleaming like black enamel, as if they were brand-new. My father always took good care of his own footwear and he used to tell me to keep heels in good repair, as they were the last that anyone saw of you.

Such things lodge in the mind, only to surface many years later. In later years, King George VI invited me to join the Army and while I was malingering there as an indispensable cog in maintaining Britain as a third-rate power, everyone took a turn of guard duty. The best turned-out soldier was awarded the 'stick' and was excused the temptations of guardhouse cocoa at three in the morning. I always won it, thanks in no small measure to boots that gleamed like big bright beetles. That uncharacteristic surge of activity on my part must have escaped the notice of my comrades detailed for duty for they took it philosophically that none of them was going to win the stick. And in later years, when I used to meet the late Lady McMillan, she would greet me with, "Ah, here comes the man with the shiny shoes!"

The third memory was of an incident that could have been fatal. We were out with friends of my parents and had gone to the Bishopton Hotel. Drivers in those days thought nothing of drinking and driving. On the way home in the dark, on a wet night, with my father at the wheel, the car somersaulted several times and ended up in a field. Miraculously, no one was killed, nor even seriously injured. When we got home, eventually, my father discovered that he'd lost his house keys and he had to borrow a large, heavy poker and prise the door open.

The last incident that I remember from this time brought home to me the existence of class and snobbery, and although I was aware that something unpleasant was happening, naturally the ramifications meant nothing. I used to play with some children at Oakshaw and it was possible to play under the street lamps in safety. Only two girls were there on one occasion, including a fair-haired girl with a long neck which had caused someone to nickname her 'the Swan'. Her manners, though, were strictly Ugly Duckling. She was also at the J.N.I, but her parents were, unlike mine, most likely middle-class professional people. The stratifications of class were much more evident then than today and this little girl unfortunately had been brought up to reflect the opinions of her parents. I recall her saying to the other, dark haired girl, "This is a game that only two can play."

TENEMENT SYMPHONY

Many of you might have only a vague idea, or even none at all, of what a tenement is. They tend to be thought of as some species of high-rise flat. A tenement is a building of two or more storeys. Normally they are to be found in what I suppose could be called terraces, although huffy ones have been known to stand on their own. The one that I lived in, No. 47, is part of a terrace of seven blocks, 45 to 57, all four-storeys and around 60 to 65 feet high. The entrance to each tenement is through a communal close and as you walk to the end there is a house on the left. Turn right and there is the middle house and facing you is the third dwelling. Immediately to the left is the stair. If you turn second left, this takes you past the communal lavatory for the ground-level dwellers, through the door and into what was commonly called the backdoor, with its drying green. To the left of the green was a row of coal bunkers standing back to back with those of No. 45. Then there was a bay with two bins, like giant pram bodies, with long carrying poles. It took two men to lift a bin. At the top left-hand corner stood the brick-built wash house, which had a slate roof. Inside was a brick fireplace and huge copper boiler and a plunging pole about the size of Samson's cudgel. A U-shaped chimney carried the smoke out. There was also the 'mangle' - a giant wringer with two rubber rollers, which looked as if it had been designed by Torquemada. Manufactured by Acme, this fearsome apparatus was operated by a big cast-iron handle and you could have fed an elephant through it without too much effort. Every householder had allocated times in which to use the wash house and back green and there was a lot of co-operative washing. (No, I don't mean the P.C.M.S...). The tenement was in fact a little community of its own; the shared facilities meant that twelve families had to learn how to live together in harmony, and generally, in our block, we did.

Back inside and up the stairs there was a lavatory on the half-landing that was kept rigorously clean. The wall was white-washed and white lines were painted along the floor. There was a batch of torn-up pieces of newspaper, often on a string, and what fun that dear little advertising puppy would have had there! I am told that there was usually also what was called a Kelly lamp, but I don't remember it. Up a few more stairs and there were three more houses. The middle houses, of course, had no windows to the back. If you took a deep breath and kept on climbing, you reached the top where there was a dizzy view from the stairhead window.

Each tenement had its queen and as befitting a queen, ours resided in the left-hand house at the top. She was Mrs Andrews, a genial lady with glasses. She was kind, wordly-wise and could always be relied upon to provide help and advice. She also provided what we shall delicately refer to as 'medicinal compounds'! In those days, doctors cost money. Another kindly and senior lady, Mrs McKenzie, lived in the middle house. Occasionally she gave me a bath in the copper boiler. Living in a tenement, you were never lost for friends - there were eleven families of them.

Apart from keeping you fit - and you had to be - living on the top storey had the twin advantages of no one above you and much less traffic in the hallway and therefore it was an easier job to keep the place clean. Pity the poor old coalman, though.

A TENEMENT DWELLING

The house in which I lived was one up, on the left. The front door faced on to what was termed the 'landing', and once through the front door entry to the house was by a short hall. To the right, off an even shorter hall, was the bedroom fronting on to the street. I recall sitting at the window in this room, suffering from an excruciating cramp in a leg and watching the subdued V.J. Day celebrations at the Caledonia Cafe across the street, on the corner of Blythswood Drive. To the left of the hall was the living room. In here, immediately to the left, was a box bed, recessed in the wall. The front of this recess naturally was open, although a curtain was hung and could be drawn if desired. It was a cosy nook. To the right of the door was another box bed. I spent many hours convalescing in those beds, suffering from the likes of toochache, and sometimes from jaundice. For that ailment I was attended to by *Mister* - not Doctor - Millar, one of the town's leading medical practitioners, who had his surgery in Orr Square. I looked like a cross between Charlie Chan and Fu Manchu and it was either for jaundice or measles that I was sent to the Infectious Diseases Hospital at Bridge Street, known as the Bladda (after the bladdawort that grew in profusion around the area). Parents were not allowed in to visit; instead they gathered below an upstairs window where their children were waiting and were forced to talk to the inmates from the street. Such a scene, at night under the lamp-light, sticks in my mind. The Bladda can be seen on postcards of Paisley.

Resplendent and resembling a beached battle cruiser, the kitchen range commanded the end wall of the living room. The range was made of cast iron, and according to Paisley historian David Rowand was likely to have been made at the Carron Iron Works in Falkirk or at Smith & Welstood at Bonnybridge. The door hinges of the oven and other fittings were of steel. The range was an all-purpose piece of heating and cooking equipment, with a central fireplace and compartments with doors on either side, where baking and roasting could be done. There were several trivets for sitting the kettle or pots on. There was a surround of tiles or embossed paper, I can't remember which, and along the top of the range was a mantelpiece with a brass rail underneath, which could be used to dry washing. A filthy con-coction called black leading was used to clean and placate the monster and once the job was done it radiated a muted but magnificent gun-metal gleam. The range was the focal point of the room and was especially wel-coming during winter nights.

In the back wall of the kitchen, beside a window looking out on to the backdoor, was the entrance to the tiny scullery. There was a window above the sink, with a space for stacking the dishes after washing. The sink might initially have been of black cast-iron but I know that later we had a white sink. To the left as you entered the scullery was - wait for it - a coal bunker and above it cupboards for food and dishes. I can visualise today's young housewives fainting away in disbelief. The lid of the bunker lifted up and part of the front, also hinged, came down. The coal that we got, tipped out of hundredweight bags, was a sparkling inky black, probably washed Welsh anthracite. My Grandma Gunn, from Barngill (or Burngill, the names seemed to be interchangeable) in Bridge of Weir, once commented that we'd all eat a pickle of dirt before we died. So if I swallowed any coal dust, it didn't do me any harm. Nor, come to think of it, did the dense fogs or Paisley's smoky atmosphere. (Does anyone remember making coal flowers? You put some pieces of coal in a bowl and poured over various ingredients which reacted with the coal and produced a variety of 'flowers' in vibrant colours.*)

9

There we were - Mother, Father, me, the dog and Sooty the cat, a feline rogue, given, amongst other escapades, to clawing up one side of the neighbours' sheets and down the other with easily imaginable results. Eventually, Fate, in the shape of someone's boot, caught up with him and he had to be put down.

However, we didn't always have the house to ourselves. A favourite way of supplementing income in those days was to take in lodgers, but there was one I didn't like. He was unctous and sly, like a fugitive from a Dickens novel, and eventually my parents came to feel the same way and he got his marching orders. The other one whom I can remember was a young, likeable Aberdonian. He was a very heavy smoker at a time when that was nothing exceptional. Sitting in his armchair one day, he drew on his cigarette, blew the smoke through a spotless white handkerchief and left a deep brown-black stain on the linen and a deeper impression on my mind. My own flirtation with smoking was brief and nauseatingly unpleasant and instead I decided to debauch myself on cinnamon sticks and fruitcake ends from the baker across the street.

Looking back, I realise that there were some peculiar aspects of tenement living. For example, although you knew everyone in your own building, you were more friendly with some than with others. And only a few of the people who were living in the adjacent closes were known - other buildings and their occupants might as well have been on another street. Our patch ran from 47 to 57 and there was one member of our clique in 37. There was no one from the other side of the road, or from Blythswood Drive, which runs east, alongside the Fountain Gardens. Andrew Street also runs east and from the Caledonia Street end we also had a few friends. Three came from the Greenock Road/Murray Street area, near the junction with Caledonia Street. The names of the families that I can remember in 47 were McNab, Hillier, Wylie, Bell, McConnell, Edwards, Andrews and McKenzie.

*Coal Flowers Recipe

Ingredients:

1 tablespoon of Prussian Blue	1 tablespoon of coloured ink
3 tablespoons of household ammonia	3 tablespoons of cold water
2 tablespoons of common salt	

Method

Put small pieces of coal in bowl. Mix the ingredients together and pour on coal. Leave in a warm place and every 2 or 3 days pour small amounts of salt dissolved in water down the side of the bowl into the mixture until the 'flowers' bloom.

CHEWING GUM, VIMTO AND STIRRING LOINS

My friends and I did not belong to anything as grand and organised as a gang. It would be more accurate to describe us as merely a group with common interests. Our members were, in no special order, Benny and his cousin Robert, Harry and Charlie (brothers), Billy, Sammy and his younger brother, Alasdair or Alistair, Bobby and Jimmie (brothers), Eddie, Joe, Adam - a bit older and not much involved with most of our activities – another Robert, also in this category, Ian and his younger brother, and Betty, May and Helen, the latter two again peripheral. Three of these friends were Catholics, but beyond knowing that they went to different schools from us, the label meant nothing. Anyone of a delicate disposition should skip the next few paragraphs.

We knew nothing of drugs in those days and for us Vimto and Tizer was as strong as the drink got. Chewing gum became popular during the war after the Americans arrived. We got gum and the older girls got nylons (and per-haps also an unwanted pregnancy). Such was our tenacity in the search for gum that occasionally it introduced us to some rather unusual scenes. Once, some of us came upon an American and a local lady 'cementing' Anglo-American relations in the Fountain Gardens and, undeterred, Jim-mie went up and asked for gum! "Any gum, mister?" was the time-honoured phrase and the American, hardly missing a stroke, threw Jimmie a wad before suggesting to him where he might then go. Discarded con-doms were a common sight in the Gardens and at that time notions of a sexual nature were developing in our young minds as well.

Betty was the interest that most of us had in common. She was one of the boys, although, as we soon discovered - being of an observant turn of mind on occasion - she was a somewhat different shape from us. Dark-haired (my type ever since, so maybe there is something in the theory of the influ-ence of first contacts), Betty had slightly-protruding teeth and wasn't a rav-ishing beauty. Not that this bothered us, however, as she was both pleasant and very democratic. She dispensed her favours to all, sometimes for free, sometimes for comics, and that was the kind of barter system we liked.

Before the vice squad batters the door down, let me expand on those naughty statements. It wasn't until years later, when I had really mastered the reading of joined-up writing, that I first came across the expression 'breasts like melons'. But Betty had them . . . . To say that she initiated us

11

into the dark mysteries and joys of sex would be rather pompous and untrue - it was much too innocent, unsophisticated and sometimes funny for that. The girl didn't know anymore than we did. She liked us, we liked her, and it was all great fun. (Some of the comics weren't bad, either.) I recall that her brassiere resembled an American football player's protective harness and that when she was touched, her skin went taut as a drum.

However, nothing ever happened beyond fumbled groping (how apposite that word is!). If marked on ice dancing terms, the highest mark would have been about 3 out of 10. It was only much later, when life's kaleidoscope had scattered us, that we discovered the really serious facts of life - for instance, that the girls danced backwards. Betty was one of us and we didn't take advantage of our own. And, looking back with affection, I realise that none of us ever thought that she was cheap or talked of her in a derogatory way. She wasn't a topic of conversation. That was for important things, like football.

Tenement closes were perfect for those juvenile explorations. Some of them had doors and occasionally one of the boys would keep a look-out while another was permitted entry to the Promised Land. I don't quite know what I expected the first time, if anything, and I had to be prompted by both the look-out *and* the willing maiden; I recall little about it but it must have been safe and pleasurable sex. Evidently stamp collecting didn't destroy or stunt my sex life and if we'd even heard of the word orgasm, we would have thought, vaguely, that it was either a recital of church music or a riot at the YWCA. What I *do* remember is the exact close in which it happened. On occasion, I've walked by and had a private chuckle. Betty used to tease us at times, so we were all learning. That she had a crush on two of the lads didn't diminish her democratic tendencies, I'm glad to say. Eventually, much to our sorrow, she emigrated with her family somewhere south of Capricorn. So Betty, wherever you are … thanks for the mammaries.

A THING OF BEAUTY . . .

. . . or why I didn't play for Saints and Scotland. Despite the attractions Betty had to offer, football was our main pastime. Had an alert director - if such a paragon ever existed - leaned over the wall at Love Street, he would have seen several brilliant footballers. Most of the time we played with a tennis ball, or 'tanner ba' as we called it. The great Sir Stanley Matthews has related how he and his chums played with a tennis ball because they couldn't afford a proper football. It taught them intricate ball control and anyone who has seen the likes of Matthews play (wonderful memories, even when he was carving up the Scottish defence) will appreciate the skill involved.

Some of the boys could do everything except make it sit up and beg. Wee Jimmie not only had magic feet, he was also King of the Heidies. There was a suitable wall at the corner of Caledonia Street and Andrew Street, and with palms flat on the smooth surface, Jimmie kept that ball going until you might have thought that it was actually running up and down a track between head and wall. Charlie was another with the talent. He was tall and thin, like a pipe cleaner with hair, and he waved his hands about like a demented policeman on points duty with such mesmerising effect that we were so busy watching the gyrations that we lost sight of what he was doing with the ball.

You've heard the expression 'two left feet'. I wasn't even that good and really had little talent, but sometimes I scored a lucky goal. I was for a time a member of the Wallneuk U.M. team, which was duff. With me in it, that wasn't surprising and I sometimes thought that the coach was carrying Christian charity too far until we changed our strip to green and white hoops, and we had a run of success. (This strip was also used by a professional team that still plays today, although for the life of me I just can't recall their name.) Disaster quickly followed, however, when two of our best players, brothers, emigrated. Our first game after they left saw us tanked 8 - 0. Somehow, I don't think that I was cut out for the Big Time. Now and again we played teams from other nearby areas, such as the so-called Glen Street Gang - a bunch of sawn-off James Cagneys - in what were really formalised, ineffectual 'gang' fights, usually eleven-a-side, but numbers optional.

The thing of beauty? That was the football itself. Made up of leather panels, quite often in T-shape, by a firm called Thompson, they were expertly stitched into one of the few deadly weapons that wasn't banned by the Geneva Convention. Inside the leather cover was a rubber bladder with a small tube and a bicycle pump with a special nipple adapter was used to pump it up. Then it was laced. When new, it was a beautiful piece of craftsmanship (or possibly the balls were made by women workers?) with a rich, rotund gleam of top-quality leather. Kicking one wasn't easy, especially in damp conditions. I wonder what present-day footballers, with their light, ballerina boots, would make of it.

You had to keep the ball dubbined. Like blackleading, dubbin might have been invented at Portland Down. Our nickname for the ball was a 'cudger', origin unknown; I once wrote to a psychologist who was collecting and researching into the derivation of vernacular words, but she could provide no clues. As it got older and more worn, the cudger resembled an expired haggis, but if your head connected with the laced-up part, you knew something about it, or not, as the case may be.

In those days, we knew nothing of violence on the field or off, except, perhaps, for the manly mayhem at Love Street. When I was quite young, my father would take me to see the Saints, but I spent most of the time searching for colourful cigarette packets such as Players, Capstan, Gold Flake, Craven A and Black Cat, with their equally colourful contents, the much sought-after card. These were wonderful objects with perhaps the design of a fearsome inhabitant of some faraway land, the workings of railway carriage couplings or a majestic ship of the line. Frequently, myself and other small boys would wander off, in perfect safety, end up lost, and our parents would be invited to claim us at the office where we had been taken by a kindly policeman. There was always a ripple of laughter in the ground when this was announced over the tannoy. To return to my tack, no one carried weapons and no one was ever mugged or assaulted. There were the usual fist fights which were as trivial as their causes, a part of growing up that left no scars, physical or mental.

In fact, the biggest threat to law and order was the local police Inspector, Mr Lyle, a red-haired giant, as all the constabulary members seemed to be. Football was banned in the streets and occasionally we played on a piece of waste ground at the far end of Andrew Street, behind Gillespie's Garage, which fronted on to Love Street. But usually our games took place in the street and Lyle made a career of hounding us at every opportunity. Caught loitering, no doubt with intent, was another dire offence and we would be herded in the big, blue police box in Greenock Road, just round the corner from Albion Street. Our parents had to come and procure our release. In those days the police had it easy.

Our other activities included marbles, roller skating -sometimes on the pathways at the Abbey - submarines in a row of slate bin sheds with holes in the roofs (that is, going inside the sheds and sticking a wooden pole through their rotting roofs and pretending that we were using a periscope), tying doorknobs together with string, chap-door-run and the milk bottle top game. The tops of the bottles were of cardboard, about one and a half inches in diameter, with a small press-out disk in the middle to permit milk to be poured without removing the whole top. The skill in the game lay in trying to flick a top as near to a wall as possible from a certain distance. My other great enthusiasm, one which turned out to last a lifetime, started when I swapped a large bag of marbles for a pile of stamps; that was me hooked on collecting in general and philately in particular.

A very popular pastime was going to the cinema. Paisley had eight cinemas and I would go on my own or with my parents or friends. Three of the four principal halls were in the High Street: the Regal was opposite the Coats Memorial Church and the Picture House and the La Scala were farther along, nearer the Cross. All were on the south side of the street, probably because building sites were available there. The Kelburne - now the only cinema left in the town - is out on the Glasgow Road, not far from the Grammar School.

Films, mainly American, were the entertainment of the masses and the halls were packed six days a week. Almost inevitably queuing had to be endured, especially for the 'last house'. I can still visualise the High Street at the La Scala on a rainy night, the street black and shining like a whale's back, the buildings ablaze with light and tram cars clanging by like run-away Christmas trees past a huddled queue of people that snaked away round the corner into St Mirren Brae. The rain was a good reason, if any were needed, to cuddle your current lady love.

Then came the moment when we gained shelter under the canopy and could actually see the ticket cubicle. After that, it was a matter of patience and soon we were inside, bag of sweets in hand, shown to our seats by the usherette and about to be transported, courtesy of Hollywood, to imaginary worlds.

A full programme was usually two films, one A and one B, a cartoon, news, trailers of coming attractions, and advertisements. Female assistants

15

patrolled with trays of calories such as ice cream and fruit drinks and as always there was a rush during intervals.

When a film was actually showing, spirals of blue smoke drifted by the screen to the ceiling. It was like a Red Indian convention. One time when I was with friends, I took a cigarette. I quickly became dizzy and wasn't quite sure where I was, but when I came to I decided once again that there would be no more smoking for me.

The High Street cinemas and the Kelburne were well-ordered places. But the likes of the Palladium down the pend off High Street and the Astoria in Lawn Street, on the site of the former roller skating rink, were more down market, cheaper and much noisier. The latter, known as the Flea Pit, had us 'itching to get in and scratching to get out'. They showed serials and these were the highlights of the programme, in which the mainly young audience participated with gusto. Both cinemas had a mixture of seats and benches.

On one occasion I went to the New Alex, up Neilston Road, opposite the entrance to the former Royal Alexandra Infirmary. I was late in getting there so I had to sit in the front row. Pack-em-in was the motto and I was so near to the screen that I got a crick in the neck. Despite the feeling that it was all going to topple down on top of me, *Rhapsody in Blue* with Robert Alda (the father of Alan of *M*A*S*H* fame), was wonderful and one of the gems in my record collection is a 12" disc of the music, with Paul Whiteman and his Orchestra accompanied by George Gerswhin at the piano.

Another Saturday, I went to the pictures twice. The second cinema I visited that day was the West End and I saw Errol Flynn and Basil Rathbone in *The Adventures of Robin Hood*. This featured perhaps the most exciting sword duel in cinema, although those in *The Prisoner of Zenda, The Mark of Zorro* and *Scaramouche* run it close. As usual, Claude Rains was stealing scenes and there was a thrilling score by Erich Wolfgang Korngold, which won him an Academy Award. With films as good as this one of the favourite ploys to get our money's worth was to stay and see the programme the second time around, but the management eventually got wise to that.

The other magnet of entertainment was Paisley Theatre in Smithhills. My parents went regularly to the cinema on Tuesdays, probably because it was the local half-holiday, and invariably on Saturday evenings we attended the

Caledonia Street, looking north. At the mid-right is the Fountain Gardens, while St Mirren Park is near top-right. MacKean's chimney is centre-left.

The street, looking north, 1930s. All the buildings on the right-hand side are long gone and the granite setts ('causies') were removed after the War. Our favourite sweetie shop, run by Annie Howatt, was near the lamp-post.

My house on Wellmeadow Street was No.30 in the two-storey tenement with the central chimney on the far right. The dome, top-left, belongs to the John Neilson.

Glen Street runs east to west between Love Street and Caledonia Street. The man at the right is James Nicholson, of No.13.

The junction of St James's Street and Love Street, c.1946, with cocooned American Grumman Avenger monoplanes on their way back to the States via Glasgow.

St James's Street was laid in the 1830s at the same time as Caledonia Street and Glen Street. The Holy Trinity Church is at the eastern end of the street, together with the Sheriff Court.

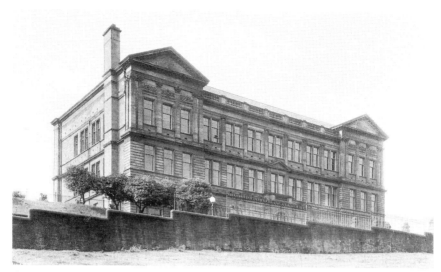

Camphill School. Camphill Brae was opposite my mother's shop on Canal Street. There were tenements on both sides and behind them stood the school.

The Neilson Institution, or J.N.I., and Camphill faced each other across the town like doughty champions of education. The school, a short climb from Wellmeadow up West Brae, is now converted into flats. The episode with 'the Swan' took place at the right of the picture.

Theatre, our seats having been booked in advance. I preferred to have a view looking down on the stage. Most of the famous entertainers came to Paisley and I recall Lex McLean and Tommy Morgan and the Short Family which included Jimmy Logan and Annie Ross. In the past international stars such as Chaplin and Pavlova performed in Paisley. The Theatre backed on to the River Cart and there are stories about the dressing rooms flooding.

My memories of the Regal centre mainly around the organ, played by Doris Bamford. It was magic to watch this leviathan, festooned with coloured lights, rising up out of the floor with Miss Bamford, a petite blonde lady, playing with one hand and waving with the other - Paisley's answer to Ethel Smith. Miss Bamford lived in a house quite near to the cinema and gave music lessons. The tradition of music in the cinema goes back to the beginning - 1895 - when someone hit upon the idea of employing a pianist whose job it was to interpret the action on the screen. Some venues had full orchestras and the advent of sound in 1929 put most of the musicians out on the street. The mighty Wurlitzers and Hammonds came in during the 1930s and until the '60s kept going a link to the birth of Cinema which no longer exists.

ADULTS AND THE WAR

Naturally, we knew that adults existed, but they inhabited another world that had little to do with ours. We were at the stage that most children go through, when they think of their parents as none too bright and only there for their convenience. Little did we realise the trials and tribulations that parents endured, doing their best in often difficult circumstances and seldom, if ever, being appreciated for their troubles. In fact, expecting appreciation probably never entered their minds. Wartime simply exacerbated their problems, but the fact that we all survived proves that they could and did improvise, coping with various privations and making us stronger for the experience. For instance, I can recall being in the house of Jimmie and Bobby and watching their father, surrounded by his set of lasts and tools and repairing their footwear. During the War, I don't ever remember being ill-clothed or cold or inadequately fed. I like to think that perhaps we eased things a little by not getting up to anything too serious.

At that time, one of the popular activities in our part of the street (and probably elsewhere) was the back door concert held in the summer. They were efficiently organised and as many people as possible were encouraged to participate. Potential participants couldn't always be relied upon, of course. I was down to sing a popular ballad, 'South of the Border (Down Mexico Way)'. The back door of No. 47 was mobbed. I took one look and got cold feet. As with football, show business wasn't for me. This episode had a sad ending. At the top of No. 45 lived a lady, who I think was an invalid. I don't know how the news of my refusal got around, but I was invited up to see the lady who asked me to sing the song to her. With all the insensitivity of the young - tempered, maybe, by an element of panic and nerves - I again refused. Shortly afterwards she died and I have never forgotten the incident.

SEASIDE MEMORIES

One of my parents' favourite regular summer activities was going on one of the weekly runs by Young's Buses to many parts of Scotland. Almost every Sunday we would gather, along with many other buddies, at the garage in Gordon Street, where I would admire the cream and red leviathans. While I know that I visited lots of places, I can remember very little of them. One trip that I do recall was to the Inveraray area. We left the bus to walk about in the sunshine (yes, it was always sunny then) and we came to a farm. The farmer happened to be leaning on the gate and at his side was a calf that had not been long-born. My parents got to talking, the farmer asked my name and that's how the bovine branch of the family got started.

Holidays to the coast were always anticipated with glee and we were usually either at Largs or Loop Cottages, which are still there, between Chapelton Point, just out of Seamill, and Ardrossan. On the ground at either side of the Cottages were a collection of holiday homes, mostly caravans, on permanent sites. Ours was somewhat different. The main part of the home was an old Lanarkshire tram body dating from the late 1930s. It still had its original long windows and leather seats running along the sides. On the front was built a small kitchen, while a bedroom was connected to the back. A few yards away stood the sea wall. Jump over that and you were on the sand with the sea stretched out before you. From the beach you could see the skeletal remains of a wreck - still there - and a little way out was a rocky outcrop where seals played. On the horizon lay Arran and to the left, Ardrossan.

I think that the Cottages were rented, rather than owned, and during our time the occupants were Willie and Mary Dale. Willie was quite tall and dark, with the detached ways of a man who spent most of his time outdoors. He was a mole catcher and he used to show me his catch of little furry corpses on a string. I'm sure that I wasn't very enthusiastic, although perhaps my mother was as Willie made her a moleskin cape. Mary was plump and jolly and she ran a little shop within the cottages which provided us with the daily necessities. Mary was also the organiser of the sandcastle competitions and she would march along the beach judging the entries. Also great fun were the night-time barbecues on the beach, with several big fires, like beacons, reaching into the indigo sky. Mary was the chief of these festivities.

On one occasion, when my parents had gone home, I stayed on with Mary and Willie. I was to sleep in a small narrow room which had a quaintly pointed roof made entirely of glass panes. I stood on the bed as Mary helped me on with my pyjamas. I was missing my parents and the tears were rolling down my cheeks, and to try and take my mind off my sorrows Mary cajoled me to sing 'Ten Green Bottles' with her. Away in the distance the lights of Ardrossan floated like a galaxy.

We usually stayed a month during the school holidays, sometimes with the Mitchell family from 45 Canal Street. The two fathers came for a fortnight and I have a photograph of mine with his Rover saloon up on the main road. The Mitchell children were Margaret and Bobby. He was deaf and dumb, but alert and intelligent. We brought out the worst in each other and in one escapade, I laid some of his lead soldiers at the edge of the table and chopped their heads off. He immediately got the idea that he'd do the same to me and I had to scarper as he grabbed a knife. Another time was very unpleasant for me and sorry, Saltcoats, this is my only memory of you. I had probably been stuffing myself and got diarrhoea. Our parents were away somewhere. Bobby did his best to get me to the lavatories, but I was too miserable with discomfort to help myself and the worst happened.

In small boy fashion, when at Loop Cottages, I'm sure that I didn't wash myself for a whole month. All I did was put on a bathing costume in the morning, jump over the wall and run to the sea. As for rain - never heard of it.

I had my first inkling of what violent death was while I was on holiday. There was a road accident near the Cottages. What stuck in my mind, and still does, is seeing the horribly fascinating pools of blue-black blood drying on the road in the summer sunshine.

West Kilbride is near the Cottages, but I only have two memories of the place. Today, the sad remains of the little cinema can still be seen and it was there that I saw the original *Treasure Island* starring Wallace Beery as Long John Silver and Jackie Cooper as Jim Hawkins. There used to be a chemist in the main street - a newsagent is now in the premises - and I can remember one window stacked up with Dinky toys in their distinctive yellow boxes. The big patch of colour was visible from quite a distance away and naturally it drew little boys towards it like a magnet.

Treasure Island must have had a big effect on me. How else can I account for my depredation of the Largs boating pond with my large yacht, yellow with a green trim, called *The Yellow Maurader* and the terror of the other yacht owners. The hull is still in the loft; so much for piratical predilections.

The other Largs memories are a rag-bag: concerts in the Barrfields; the old cinema, where they used to play Bing Crosby singing 'Beautiful Dreamer' and 'Where the Blue of the Night (Meets the Gold of the Day)'; playing in the carcass of a Sunderland at the flying boat slipway; cadging crumpled Ceylon stamps and coins from returning soldiers billeted at *The Moorings;* going to the swanky new Viking cinema; and meeting, in the Haylie Hotel, a man in his eighties who had all his own teeth! Didn't I live a full life?

PUZZLING BEHAVIOUR

As I have said, for most of my childhood parents just seemed to be there, vaguely hovering somewhere in the background. They were never a topic of discussion; we had more important things to talk about and to do. But sometimes adult actions impinged on our cocooned lives. At the time that we moved to Caledonia Street, around 1938, I was at the John Neilson School. Once, when I was absent with some illness or minor mishap, the

School Attendance Officer was at the door at mid-day to find out the reason, which had to be an acceptable one. My teacher was Miss Noble, a lady of heroic stature. One day we were walking along Caledonia Street and she ensured that I walked on the outside, as that's what a gentleman did. I've never forgotten that, or by extension, Miss Noble, and a gallant attitude towards women is the result.

My father had attended Camphill Secondary School, one of the three important schools in Paisley, the Grammar being the third; it was non fee-paying. I would be about nine when the bombshell landed. My father decided that I was to be taken out of the J.N.I. and sent to Camphill. It had been good enough for him, so it would be good enough for me, not that I had any say in the matter. Naturally, I wasn't privy to any of the shenanigans that this decision ignited, although I remember Miss Noble visiting the house. It wasn't merely a rain of trouble that fell into my life, more like a deluge. At that time, the course of a pupil's life and career depended on the Qualifying Examination - the 'qualie' - taken at around eleven years of age. Before I could get to Camphill, I would first have to go to a primary school for the intervening period. Had I stayed at the Neilson, then I would have gone through to the senior stage without all the disruption.

The school was Mossvale, a red sandstone building in Shortroods, one of the tougher areas of Paisley. I wonder if my father ever gave a thought to the effect that all this was going to have on me. One day I was wearing the uniform of a prestigious school, the next day I was roughing it. Some of the pupils, as I soon discovered, were, amongst other things, mean, aggressive and devious. Many of the girls were even worse. As a new lad, I was an automatic target for the would-be bullies. However, I was big for my age, a factor in my favour as they might have been tempted to go further than they were capable of, which proved so in one case. I don't rouse easily but one day I followed Sam Goldwyn's advice and 'retaliated first'. Things were fine after that and I remember one lad, Tom Peacock, making comments of approval, even although the other lad wasn't feeling too good. A more subtle bully was a big red-haired thug called Jeffries who never actually resorted to the bare knuckles approach. He favoured the psychological needle, never thrust in quite far enough in to trigger a violent response from me. He would have fitted in very cosily in the Gestapo. Maybe he was a coward at heart, as such types often are, but I was afraid of him for a time. I like to think that he got his come-uppance somewhere. Then again, maybe a good punch on the nose would have saved him some future grief, who knows.

It was Tom Peacock who discovered that, apparently, I had only hazy notions about the alphabet, which was probably true, being, as I related, lazy. He told the teacher, which did me a favour, although I don't think that's what he intended, even if he wasn't a malicious boy. However, ridicule can be a sharp weapon. Still, I can console myself - they say that Einstein wasn't much good at arithmetic and that Fred Astaire was an indifferent ballroom dancer.

My teacher at Mossvale was Miss Watson - one of the significant people in my life - and she took a shine to me. Evidently, as with Miss Marr in the Neilson, she saw perceptively that there was something in my head, if only she could coax it out. And she did, to the extent that I passed the vital examinations and went to Camphill. My arithmetic was a few degrees worse than Einstein's and a boy called Gordon Graham, who lived near Barnsford Bridge, was very helpful. Another pupil who could have gone to Camphill was Tom Cunningham, as he gained the necessary marks. He decided not to do so, or, more likely, his family decided for him. Tom had a great artistic gift. I was good in that line but he had the magic and I hope that his talent was developed.

Despite the ructions caused, ending up at Camphill, instead of remaining at the Neilson, had happy results. I liked the school. I had teachers such as Wee Nap (maths), Cowboy Kate - who swayed from the perpendicular to the sublime - and the two Stevensons, one called the Forty-five because he always inclined a pupil's head at 45 degrees before giving it a belt that took it almost to the horizontal. There was also the Fifteen, The Masher (Mr Johnson, whose permanent five o'clock shadow added to his menace), Messrs Dow and Chalmers - the Technical teachers, Heckie Fraser, whose secret weapon was a glass eye as no one ever knew who he was actually looking at, and finally, a significant teacher from my personal point of view, Thomas McCrossan, my English teacher in the senior years.

As with Miss Marr and Miss Watson, he knew that there was something in me waiting to be drawn out. He encouraged my incipient writing skills, which were gradually revealing themselves in essays, and helped me to develop my imagination. He imparted to me a love of language, one of the greatest gifts that anyone can give, and, on occasion, he imparted it in a very direct way. An accurately-flighted jotter taught me the difference between 'who' and 'whom' and I think I often disappointed him when I fell below the standards he thought I could attain.

One particular example of falling standards comes to mind. My fellow Technical studies pupil (there were only the two of us) Raymond Smith and I had heard that the fabled Moscow Dynamo were visiting Ibrox to play Rangers. They had already murdered Cardiff 10 - 1 and also beaten Arsenal and we were determined to play hookey - 'plunking' - to see them. We bought our tickets outside the ground and found the terraces mobbed. This was the match in which the famous inside-right Torry Gillick, with his trade mark shorts which reached to his knees, stood counting the Russian players and drew the referee's attention to the fact that there were twelve of them on the pitch! The result was 2 - 2 and our feet literally didn't touch the ground when the crowd surged out of the park. That was 1945 or '46. I can't recall what our punishment was, but it must have been worth it.

Talking of significant people, I should mention here Robert (Bert) Skinner, a friend of my parents, who lived in Caledonia Street. Among other things, Bert had been in the Indian Army and he related to me the story of an inter-regimental football match, held on a suitable patch of ground, with about a quarter of a million spectators massed on the surrounding hillsides! When he returned to Britain, he and two others were offered terms by Celtic but he didn't accept. But there were other options open to him as he was that time's equivalent of a polymath. He qualified as an accountant and after he went to stay in Kilbarchan, I went in one day and there he was, making his own three-piece suite: frame, springs, leather upholstery, varnishing, the lot. As with Mr McCrossan, I was encouraged by Bert in my reading and essay-writing, which we would then discuss. One on the geography of the Middle East sticks in my mind.

Errol Flynn and I had at least two things in common: we both loved to be out in the sunlight and we regretted not having learned to play the piano. I was given the chance, but I spurned it and I have always thought of that as one of my dimmer decisions (I don't know what Mr Flynn's excuse was). Listening to a whole keyboard of gifted people playing the piano has been an interest of mine for many years, through both records and concerts. Another of my significant people lived upstairs. He was Jim McConnell, who worked on the buses. Jim had a fabulous collection of jazz recordings by all the legendary musicians. (Errol Garner is playing as I write this part.) One evening, Jim came to the door with two records under his arm. One was Meade Lux Lewis with 'Honky Tonk Train Blues' on the A side; the other was Thomas 'Fats' Waller's 'Alligator Crawl'. Jim asked me which one I would like to have. Presented with two such gems, which I was familiar with having heard them and many others in Jim's home, what a decision I had to make. I chose Meade Lux Lewis but you can imagine my joy when he presented me with both records. I still have them and they are in superb condition - Jim also taught me how to care for the discs. They were the old 78s of course and among the many records I heard at Jim's were first recordings by Frank Sinatra and Judy Garland.

Even then I was an inveterate whistler and fond of improvising and Jim encouraged me in that pastime. It still provides me with a lot of pleasure as it is the cheapest method of making my own music. An amusing spin-off from this activity is that, when I go to the local supermarket, which, mercifully, has no noise that passes for music, I whistle my way around, breaking the monotony of shopping. Occasionally, women shoppers have said how much they enjoyed the melodies and the management haven't thrown me out . . . yet. Nevertheless, not everyone has appreciated my whistling over the years. I spent one school holiday in the Sorting Office at Underwood Road where I would whistle merrily as I consigned, in my imagination, letters addressed to Barrhead or Manchester or Swansea to Casablanca, Cairo and Colombo instead. Once, while immersed in a daydream, I became aware of a strangled snarl from somewhere to my right and on locating the source, received a volley of irritable remarks. The other sorters found it funny though, and I got one or two friendly winks.

THE BLACK SIDE OF LIFE

At the beginning of this little reminiscence, I mentioned my natal proximity to H.G. Wells. I knew nothing of this until one day in the street, a malicious woman from No. 49, whom I shall not name, told me about my adoption. I was stunned by the revelation that my parents weren't my parents and I had to go and ask them about the matter, which wasn't easy for me, or for them. That was one time when the great divide between parents and child was at its widest.

In retrospect, the worst event that happened in the adult world was the suicide of a woman who lived in the street. On the day of the funeral, I was standing quite near to the car bearing away the husband and I was not, understandably, more than superficially aware of his profound grief. The street was packed with people and there was an uncanny silence, broken only by the sobbing of the women. During the long years of war some would cry again for their own loved ones who would never return.

I used to go to a fish and chip shop at the end of the street, near the junction with St James' Street. One evening, an assistant, attempting to show off before some adult customers, threw a chip in my face. I wasn't having that, particularly as it was unsalted, and I threw one back at him. That rather spoiled what he thought was a funny joke and made him look the fool he was and I think that I was banished from the premises. I can't remember what the outcome of that was when I got home. But at least I had escaped with the fish suppers.

Further adult machinations were discovered one day when I was in the grocer and confectioner across the road. This was during the war, when everything was on the ration. Smarties were around at that time and also an imitation sweet which was cruder and cheaper. I bought what I thought were Smarties and the woman behind the counter muttered, "I hope he doesn't notice the difference." And I didn't until I was out of the shop. She had substituted the cheaper sweet, but charged the Smarties price. My parents probably sorted that one out. Anyway, these two incidents always remind me just how petty people can be.

WAR

I must have heard the momentous announcement of the outbreak of war over the wireless, but it doesn't stand out in my memory; and strangely, very little of what were matters of life and death has remained in my mind. In later years, I knew what my father thought about it. He had survived the Great War. My parents, like everyone else, adapted and coped with the exigencies of wartime conditions and I did not lack for the necessities. A wooden framework and tip-up seats were built in the closes and brick baffle walls erected in front, to minimise blast, should we be bombed. We were lucky as that never happened. Other parts of the town suffered deaths and casualties from the dreaded floating mines, which, as far as I know, were actually naval mines dropped by parachute and therefore all the more frightening as there was no warning of their approach. The street ack-ack guns were sited nearby and during the Clydebank Blitz I could hear them coughing their shells into the skies, as the Heinkels, having shed their deadly loads north of the river, headed southwards over the street, pursued by our fighters. The noises of the different engines were quite distinctive. I collected shrapnel from the street and somewhere I acquired the tail fin of an incendiary bomb and painted a swastika on it. The next day I climbed to the top of the Stoney Brae and gazed across the valley to the burning town of Clydebank. We used to have a young friend there, Daisy Drake, and I often wonder what her fate was.

The events that I mainly remember from the war were some of the naval actions and the on-going Battle of Britain. The first was the pursuit, cornering and eventual scuttling of the *Admiral Graf Spee* off Montevideo, in December 1939. I also remember hearing of the sinking of the *Rawalpindi* by the *Scharnhorst,* and the similar fate dealt out to the *Jervis Bay.* Then, of course, there was the terrible sinking of the *Hood* by the *Bismark.* Other aspects of war were recorded in a folio of drawings: air battles, the Desert War, Japanese incidents, Monte Cassino (a soldier advancing, bayonet fixed and a casual cigarette dangling from his lips!) and individual aeroplanes. My drawing of the scuttled *Graf Spee* seems to have disappeared but it might turn up. A local event occurred one day when my father and I were in Allison's butcher van on the way to the Red Smiddy to deliver meat. As we were passing the aerodrome, a Spitfire came in to land and ended up on its nose.

On V.E. Night, Paisley Cross was mobbed and my most enduring memory of wartime was its end. I was there, fourteen yours old and being carried around over someone's shoulder.

*

With Art Tatum playing in the background, that seems a good a memory to stop with. I've enjoyed my trip to the past; much that I had forgotten has come back to me and much that was obscure has been clarified.

I hope that you, too, have enjoyed the journey and that it might have stimulated some of your own memories. They should always be recorded in some way. Once they are gone, it is impossible to get them back.

CALEDONIA STREET

An architect's view

In her book, *A Social Geography of Paisley,* Mary McCarthy states that 'In the Sneddon, the new streets of Saint James, Glen and Caledonia were laid out and the area built up before 1830. Wellington Street and MacDowell Street were feued for building also. However, some of the land here was commandeered for the railway line from the town to Greenock. The feus marked out in the 1839 survey did not survive when the railway was built in 1840, and only MacDowell Street remained with housing near Caledonia Street. The area became an industrial sector with the founding of two print works and a dyeworks.'

Caledonia Street itself was mainly residential, with blocks of shops, but, as the aerial photograph shows, the surrounding area was heavily industrialised, mostly on the western side. The street runs north from the west end of St James's Street and contains a surprising variety of buildings, spanning a century from the 1820s to the 1920s. Some of the structures are attractive in design and construction and one is outstanding. Seen through the eye of an architect, the street begins to speak with a language that has an element of poetry in it, and takes on a dimension not normally accessible to the layman.

With David Rowand, noted Paisley historian and author, I walked north on the left (west) side of the street, from the junction with Underwood Road and St James's Street. No. 3 is a four-storey tenement dating from the 1890s, built of polished ashlar - this being the name for carefully-wrought stone - with bow pedimented windows. With the next group of buildings, we begin to step back in time. No. 5 is mid-Victorian (c.1840-50), of three storeys with a symmetrical facade. The stone is coursed ashlar - horizontally grooved - and possibly polished, but it is so weathered that it is difficult to tell. There is a symmetrical door piece, stone pilastered, and five bays (windows), double-hung. The next building, No. 7, is similar to No. 5, in grey ashlar, but with two differences: the door piece has a stone-moulded projecting cornice and there is a turret wheel stair, a stylish feature. The Alamo Pub occupies the next site, a two-storied building of 1820s vintage, with a harled finish, that is, Scottish traditional roughcast. The door pieces and windows have stone jamb surrounds. No. 9 is also of two storeys, dating from the 1820s and constructed in unpolished ashlar, chiselled and rusticated. There are four lights and a central close, which is bricked up. The present entrance has stone jambs. Of interest here is the 'Paisley pediment' at roof level. This is a triangular addition which, despite the name, is not exclusive to Paisley. I was intrigued by David's explanation that such features were added to emulate the mansions of the rich in a modest way.

The last building in this stretch, No.13, is one of the attractive structures in the street. The date on the three-storey facade tells us that it dates from 1923, so we've gone forward a hundred years. Of polished ashlar, the building has a projected central bay, with the date, and two bay windows on either side. The windows are capped with a leaded roof. Possibly there used to be a centrally-placed chimney. The gables are parapeted skew blocks. The other buildings in the stretch don't have this feature. The bottom storey is occupied by the Wellington Dairy, polished ashlar with an arched close entrance having a keystone above. The facade to the right of the door has projected eaves.

We cross Wellington Street - which is one of the shortest streets anywhere - and come to sites which are occupied by small industrial premises. No. 21 is a converted cottage from around 1830, housing the Caledonia Bar. It is of two-storeys, polished ashlar. This building also has a Paisley pediment with stone quoines and window jambs. Frontages in the 1830s were about forty feet wide on average. David commented that the older the buildings, the wider the steps were. The other enterprises here are Stanley Racing and a pizza shop. The roofs are slated, with a moulded chimney piece.

The building at No. 25 is outstanding. It is an asymmetrical three-storey structure from the 1920's of rustic Locharbriggs (Dumfries) red sandstone. The door has a moulded architrave and a tripartite keystone over the lintel. There is also a segmented or broken pediment. The feature that immediately attracts attention in the layout of the windows is a bull's eye light or oculus flanked by four keystones, giving the whole the appearance of a Maltese cross. On either side of the single window above the oculus are two lights and on the second storey, the same arrangement. The first storey has two lights to the left and five to the right. The gable is unusual, as it has six windows. The adjoining building has been demolished (and replaced by a truly grim and grimy electricity transformer station). The windows in the gable overlook what was once MacKean's Starch Works and the site is now occupied by MacKay Fabrics. A badly-sited lamp standard spoils the elevated view of the building.

Moving along the street, we come to the junction with MacDowell Street, formerly the home of A & F Craig and other industrial premises. This corner was the beginning of the 'Clayholes', Speirs, Gibb and Co., the Caledonia Fire Clay Works. The former use of the area has left its mark today at No. 37, with the evidence of subsidence and consequent cracking of the walls. The corner is occupied by a small, overgrown drying green, with four ornate cast-iron poles to support the clothes line, enclosed behind a dilapidated stone wall. The tenement, of four storeys in polished grey ashlar, dates from around 1890-1900. It has symmetrical bay windows, the central windows being in two lights and mullioned and capped with moulded pediments. In the close entrance there is an interesting feature: an elliptical arch with two cornice brackets, its likely purpose to support a transverse beam. Sadly, No. 37, where my friend Benny lived, is in a shocking state.

No. 39 is a mid-1850s three-storey tenement with a symmetrical facade in polished ashlar, five bays of windows, with shops at ground level. 41 and 43 are c.1820s, again three-storeys, with only one original window remaining. There are stone window jambs. The main feature of interest is a turret wheel stair (also present in No. 7).

The rest of the c.1890s tenements from 45 to 57, at the junction with Murray Street, are four-storey. Nos. 45 and 47 are in red sandstone, each storey divided by a moulded cornice. The lights are symmetrical, 2-3-2. I was puzzled as to why, when all the buildings in this stretch dated from around the same time, Nos. 49 to 57 were in grey ashlar. David gave a number of reasons why. Perhaps the builders had run out of an available supply of red ashlar and had to get on with the construction, using grey; or there might have been cost implications or local authority requirements. The feu superior might have wanted 45 and 47 in red or the architect might have specified the colour and material. Adding a perhaps more social reason, red might have been more acceptable to the lower middle classes, maybe MacKean's managers. Those tenements did not have 'wally' closes, i.e., tiled entrances.

Crossing the street to the junction with Albion Street, there is a small group of what must be, architecturally, among the most attractive council houses anywhere. The site here was once occupied by the Industrial School and when it was demolished around 1924, these houses were built. They are two-storey, semi-detached, with a symmetrical facade and two-light bow windows in red sandstone, the bays of which pierce the pavilion-style roof. The door pieces have bowed lintels, in keeping with the Art Deco period. External stairs give entrance to the upper storeys.

The next group of tenements, from 50 to 42, is bounded by Andrew Street and Blythswood Drive, on the south side of which runs the Fountain Gardens. The site was once occupied by the Caledonian Dye Works, possibly owned by MacKeans. The buildings are four-storey, of polished ashlar (red sandstone) and date between 1890 and 1900. The ground level is taken up with shops, as it was when I lived in the street. The asymmetrical facade is punctuated by two bow lights, with central mullions. Each storey has moulded cornicing and terminated by cast-iron ogee moulded gutters.

From the far side of the Fountain Gardens to the end of the street at the junction with St James's Street, all the old buildings have been demolished and replaced by modern housing (the postcard shows what it was once like). I also stayed in the little stretch between the Gardens and Glen Street, where, as related, Bert Skinner lived.

Caledonia Street, leading, as it does, to Greenock Road and the M8, is still a thoroughfare and likely to remain so. A walk along it will reveal the points of interest and readers of this book might be encouraged, if not to come and look at Caledonia Street, at least to inspect the buildings in their own areas. The stones tell a story.

Some historical background

1608: The first Paisley horse race, for the Silver Bells, took place. The course used was the 'four-and-twenty acres', near Underwood.

1793: The course was declared unsuitable by the Council. The new course ran along Underwood Road, Greenhill Road, Greenock Road, Murray Street ('or by the lane farther north'), Caledonia Street and back to Underwood.

The conditions stipulated that 'The riders be at the starting-post at four o'clock and run twice round the ordinary course, and afterwards to the winning-post near the south end of Caledonia Street...' The winning-post, called 'The Score', was actually in St James's Street. For a period, all entrants had to book their horses at the Saracens Head Inn, Moss Street.

1830: two brothers, weavers from Caledonia Street, won First and Second Prizes for tulips at the AGM of the Paisley Florist Society.

1846: The Corn Laws were repealed and a demonstration took place in Paisley on Monday 13th July. Instead of illuminations, it was decided that 'the decorations should consist of flowers and boughs of trees'. Lord Glasgow and other landed proprietors gave permission for the removal of superfluous branches from their woods and as soon as the Sabbath was over, thousands of people got to work and had the decorations in place by ten o'clock. 'A beautiful arch was thrown over Caledonia Street, filled with boughs, and flowers, and stuffed birds.' A procession passed under the arches at Caledonia Street, Townhead and Maxwellton Street, presumably heading for Maxwellton Park, where a meeting was held.

1848: Three Chartist meetings were held in Paisley in 1848, the third on 21st april. The people were assembled in Caledonia Street and marched through the town to a field near the Colinslee Print Works, where a Mr Ernest Jones tried to incite them to obtain and use firearms. The only occurrence was much less seditious and blood-thirsty: a Mr Robert Cochran was elected as delegate to the Convention.

1896: The Fountain Gardens, with its fine statue of Robert Burns, lies on the east side of Caledonia Street. Its existence owes much to John Love, a native of Kilmalcolm (note the third 'l'). 'That beautiful spot known as Hope Temple Gardens owing to his ardent love of landscape gardening, and from the fertility of the soil and from the best selection of plants and flowers, and trees of the rarest kind, has become one of the finest in Scotland, and is a general resort during summer.'

ACKNOWLEDGEMENTS

My special thanks to David Rowand, F.S.A. (Scot.), for his architectural insights which made Caledonia Street come alive again, and for his help with the picture selection and advice on my manuscript. To Tom Baillie, a neighbour, who identified our police nemesis and reminded me about Gillespie's Garage. To John MacMillan, General Secretary of the Rangers Social Club, for information on the Moscow Dynamo match. To Capt. Irene Houston, Capt. John Houston and the Army ladies for information on the Junior Band in the Fountain Gardens. To the sisters McNab, who stayed in No. 47 and who provided me with some useful snippets.

The top illustration on page 19 appears courtesy of R.L. Grieves, and a final thanks to Mrs. Felletti for information about her father (pictured on page 18).